# WHAT ARE IGNEOUS ROCKS?

## Molly Aloian

Crabtree Publishing Company

www.crabtreebooks.com

**Author:** Molly Aloian
**Editor-in-Chief:** Lionel Bender
**Project coordinator:** Kathy Middleton
**Photo research:** Melissa McClellan
**Designer:** Tibor Choleva
**Proofreaders:** Rachel Stuckey, Crystal Sikkens
**Production coordinator:** Margaret Salter
**Production:** Kim Richardson
**Prepress technician:** Margaret Salter

**Consultant:** Kelsey McCormack, B.Sc, M.Sc, PhD
McMaster University
**Cover:**

**Title page:** Fairy chimneys, Rose Valley, Cappadocia, Turkey

**Special Thanks:** Stu Harding, Lucyna Bethune,
Sandor Monos and Sandee Ewasiuk

This book was produced for Crabtree Publishing Company
by Silver Dot Publishing.

**Illustrations:**
© David Brock: pages 7

**Photographs and reproductions:**
© Dreamstime.com: title page (Jefras) and pages 4 (Joeygil), 10/11 large (Juliengrondin), 11 (Davinci), 19 bottom (Pljvv), 22/23 large (Winterstorm), 24 bottom left (Pancaketom), 24 bottom middle (Janhofmann), 24 middle (Knorre), 24 top (Yukosourov), 26/27 large (Kmitu), 26 top (Complexdesignpl), 27 right (duncan1890), 27 left top (Shawnhemp), 28 (Diomedes66), 29 bottom (Kinlem)

© istockphoto.com: pages: 10 middle (titine974), 12 top (meltonmedia), 14/15 large (SeppFriedhuber), 20 bottom (RoyalFive), 20 top (only_fabrizio), 20 middle (Takis_Milonas), 24 bottom right (efesan), 25 top (RuslanDashinsky), 26 bottom (Imagesbybarbara), 29 top (cfarish)

© Shutterstock.com: headline image (Peter Zurek), background image (Maxim Tupiko) and pages 4/5 large (Vulkanette), 5 (Michael Almond), 6 left (Andrea Danti), 6 right (AptTone), 8 top (my-summit), 8 large (Bonita R. Cheshier), 9 top (AridOcean), 10 top (kuma), 12/13 large (Michael Steden), 13 left (Vladimir Korostyshevskiy), 13 right (Leksele), 14 top (Kletr), 14 bottom (Kletr), 15 top (Lance Bellers), 16 bottom (Melinda Fawver), 17 top (valzan), 18 top (TechWizard), 21 top (Lorraine Kourafas), 21 bottom (jovannig), 22 bottom (Manamana), 23 left (Zelenskaya), 23 right (Martin Novak), 25 bottom (Jasenka Lukša), 25 large (Timur Kulgarin), 27 left upper middle (Martin Novak), 27 left lower middle (Linda), 27 bottom (Kirill Matkov), 28/29 large (zebra0209)

© Petr Svarc, photographersdirect.com: page 19 top

© Doug Sherman: page 17 middle

© NASA: pages 9 bottom, 12 bottom, 17 bottom

© NOAA: pages 18 bottom, 17 bottom

**Library and Archives Canada Cataloguing in Publication**

Aloian, Molly
    What are igneous rocks? / Molly Aloian.

(Let's rock)
Includes index.
Issued also in an electronic format.
ISBN 978-0-7787-7228-6 (bound).--ISBN 978-0-7787-7233-0 (pbk.)

    1. Rocks, Igneous--Juvenile literature. I. Title. II. Series:
Let's rock (St. Catharines, Ont.)

QE461.A46 2011          j552'.1          C2010-904126-7

**Library of Congress Cataloging-in-Publication Data**

Aloian, Molly.
What are igneous rocks? / Molly Aloian.
    p. cm. -- (Let's rock)
Includes index.
 ISBN 978-0-7787-7228-6 (reinforced lib. bdg. : alk. paper) -- ISBN 978-0-7787-7233-0 (pbk. : alk. paper) -- ISBN 978-1-4271-9522-7 (electronic (PDF))
1. Rocks, Igneous--Juvenile literature. 2. Petrology--Juvenile literature. 3. Magmatism--Juvenile literature. I. Title. II. Series.

QE461.A617 2010
552'.1--dc22
                                                         2010024596

# Crabtree Publishing Company

www.crabtreebooks.com          1-800-387-7650

Printed in the U.S.A./082010/BA20100709

**Published in Canada**
**Crabtree Publishing**
616 Welland Ave.
St. Catharines, Ontario
L2M 5V6

**Published in the United States**
**Crabtree Publishing**
PMB 59051
350 Fifth Avenue, 59th Floor
New York, New York 10118

**Published in the United Kingdom**
**Crabtree Publishing**
Maritime House
Basin Road North, Hove
BN41 1WR

**Published in Australia**
**Crabtree Publishing**
386 Mt. Alexander Rd.
Ascot Vale (Melbourne)
VIC 3032

# CONTENTS

# THE ORIGINS OF IGNEOUS ROCKS

There are different types of rocks on Earth. Igneous rocks are one type of rock. There are igneous rocks all over the world, and they can be different sizes, shapes, and colors. The word "igneous" comes from the Latin phrase "made from fire."

## BELOW AND ABOVE

Some igneous rocks form when **magma** below Earth's surface cools and hardens. Magma is hot melted rock.

Other igneous rocks form above Earth's surface. This happens when volcanoes erupt and shoot out **lava**. The lava hardens into igneous rock.

▶ *One type of **lava flow**, known as pahoehoe, creates a fine-grained ropy rock surface when it hardens.*

## OTHER ROCKS

✳ Metamorphic rocks and sedimentary rocks are two other types of rocks found on Earth. Metamorphic rocks are rocks that change form to become different rocks. Sedimentary rocks are made up of deposited **sediment**.

4

## COARSE AND FINE

Rocks that form deep below Earth's surface cool very slowly. The crystals have plenty of time to grow big and form coarse-grained igneous rocks.

Rocks that form on the surface cool very quickly. The crystals have no time to grow and stay small, forming fine-grained igneous rocks.

▼ This coarse-grained rock formation formed deep below Earth's surface.

◀ Magma that reaches Earth's surface during volcanic eruptions is known as lava.

# THE EARTH'S STRUCTURE

**E**arth is made up of different layers of rock. The outermost layer of Earth is called the **crust**. Below the crust is the **mantle**, which is a very thick, dense layer of rock.

## THICK LAYER

The mantle is approximately 1,800 miles (2,897 km) thick—much thicker than the crust. The outer core is the next layer. The temperature of the outer core is very hot, but the inner core is even hotter. The temperature of the inner core is over 9,000°F (4,982°C).

## GOOD TO THE CORE

(This activity needs adult supervision.)

This will give you an idea of what Earth's layers look like.

**You will need:**

- a hard boiled egg or avocado
- knife

Cut the hard boiled egg or avocado in half. Imagine that the egg yolk or avocado pit is Earth's core. The egg white or the green flesh is the mantle. Imagine that the egg shell or the avocado skin is the crust.

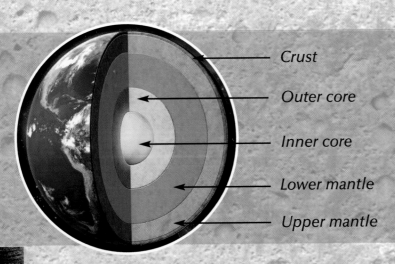

Crust

Outer core

Inner core

Lower mantle

Upper mantle

*Most diamonds are formed deep in Earth's mantle.*

## MOVING PLATES

Earth's crust is divided into giant slabs of rock called **tectonic plates**. These plates do not stay in the same place. They are constantly moving, which causes earthquakes and volcanic eruptions. They move about as fast as your finger nails grow, but the changes on Earth's surface can be enormous. For example, Iceland formed when two plates moved apart and magma rose up to fill in the gap.

## MINERAL MAKEUP

✳ Igneous rocks, sedimentary rocks, and metamorphic rocks are made up of chemicals called **minerals**. There are thousands of different minerals on Earth. Diamond, gold, and salt are examples of minerals found in rocks.

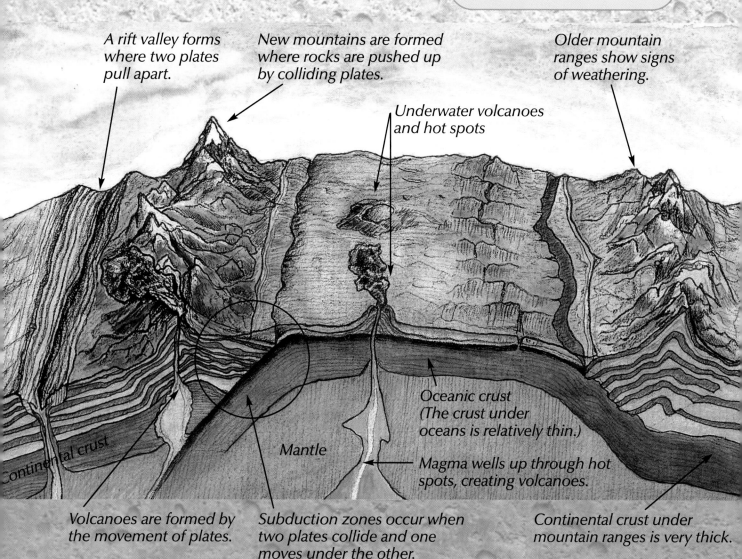

A rift valley forms where two plates pull apart.

New mountains are formed where rocks are pushed up by colliding plates.

Older mountain ranges show signs of weathering.

Underwater volcanoes and hot spots

Oceanic crust (The crust under oceans is relatively thin.)

Continental crust

Mantle

Magma wells up through hot spots, creating volcanoes.

Volcanoes are formed by the movement of plates.

Subduction zones occur when two plates collide and one moves under the other.

Continental crust under mountain ranges is very thick.

# ON THE PLATES

Earth's continents are carried on tectonic plates. They move very slowly. Volcanoes are usually found in places where the tectonic plates collide or spread apart. During a volcanic eruption, magma from inside Earth shoots out and runs down the side of the volcano.

## ON THE MOVE

Earth's tectonic plates move in three different ways. Convergent plate movement occurs when two plates slide toward each other and collide. Divergent plate movement occurs when two plates slide apart from each other. When two plates grind past each other, it is called transform plate movement.

▼ The islands of Hawaii were formed by undersea volcanic activity. There are many volcanoes in Hawaii today and we use Hawaiian words for two types of lava—"pahoehoe" and "a'a."

## MAKING A MOUNATAIN

✳ The world's tallest mountain range, the Himalayas, formed about 50 million years ago from the collision of tectonic plates.

▼ Ninety-six of the world's 100 highest mountains can be found in the Himalaya-Karakorum mountain range.

## FIERY RING

Many volcanic eruptions and earthquakes take place within an area called the Ring of Fire. This area surrounds the Pacific Ocean, where the Pacific Plate meets a number of other tectonic plates.

## NOT MY FAULT!

**Fault lines** are the spots where one tectonic plate meets another. For example, the San Andreas Fault in California is the boundary between the North American Plate and the Pacific Plate. The fault is about 810 miles (1,303 km) long.

◀ *The Ring of Fire contains 452 volcanoes caused by the movement and collisions of tectonic plates.*

▼ *The San Andreas Fault is a continental transform fault.*

# ERUPTIONS IN ACTION

Some igneous rocks form when magma erupts from a volcano as lava. The lava cools on the Earth's surface and forms igneous rocks. There are different kinds of lava that contain different minerals. An outpouring of lava caused by a volcanic eruption is called a lava flow.

## DIFFERENT VOLCANOES

There are also different types of volcanoes. Strato-volcanoes are formed from layers of lava and rock fragments. Strato-volcanoes often have snowcapped peaks. Mount Fuji in Japan is an example of a strato-volcano. Shield volcanoes have broad-shaped, gently sloping cones. Many shield volcanoes are found in Hawaii. There are many other types of volcanoes.

### HOT, HOT, HOT!

* Lava can reach up to 2,400°F (1,316°C).

▲ Mount Fuji's symmetrical cone is a symbol of Japan.

▼ Slow flowing a'a lava can destroy everything in its path.

## LOTS OF LAVA!

A'a lava is one type of lava. It does not flow very quickly. When it cools and hardens, it forms a jagged, broken, spiny surface.

Pahoehoe lava flows faster than a'a lava. When it cools and hardens, pahoehoe lava forms a smooth surface. Under this smooth surface, molten lava continues to flow, which gives the surface lava a wrinkled appearance.

Pillow lava emerges from underwater volcanoes and enters ocean water.

▼ Pahoehoe lava can create unique shapes called lava sculptures.

▼ Lava ejected into the air can create light rocks called **pumice**.

## MAKE A VOLCANO

(This activity needs adult supervision.)

### You will need:

- ½ cup water
- ¼ cup dishwashing liquid
- ¼ cup vinegar
- 2 or 3 drops of red and yellow food coloring
- clean bottle or pitcher
- ¼ cup baking soda
- small can or jar
- pile of sand or dirt

Mix the water, dishwashing liquid, vinegar, and food coloring in the bottle or pitcher. Put the baking soda into the can or jar. Outside, bury the can or jar in a pile of sand or dirt, leaving the lip of the can or jar sticking out. Pour a little of the mixture from the pitcher into the can and watch it bubble up and over—just like lava from a volcano.

The baking soda and vinegar create a gas that makes the liquid bubble up—just like the gas underground that causes the magma to rise and erupt.

# IGNEOUS ROCK FORMATION

Some igneous rocks form underground. There, magma flows into cracks, or in between layers of rock, and then solidifies. These igneous rocks are called **intrusive rocks**. Other igneous rocks form as lava cools on the surface of a volcano. These igneous rocks are called **extrusive rocks**.

## FLOORED

✳ The ocean floor is made up of an igneous rock called basalt.

▼ *Although covered by silt, basalt is the bedrock of the ocean floor.*

## MOON ROCKS!

The planets Mercury, Venus, and Mars are made mostly of igneous rock. Earth's Moon is made entirely of igneous rock.

◄ *Shown here is astronaut John W. Young walking on the Moon's surface, which is made of igneous rock.*

## INTRUSIVE AND EXTRUSIVE

Granite is an intrusive igneous rock. It is a coarse-grained rock that forms when magma cools slowly underground over thousands of years. Basalt is an extrusive rock. This fine-grained rock forms when lava cools quickly. Its minerals **crystallize** quickly. It is the most common extrusive igneous rock on Earth. Dolerite is an igneous intrusive rock with medium-sized grains.

◄ *Smooth, weathered dolerite dike at the banks of the Olifants River in South Africa*

◄ *The Rosetta Stone is a basalt fragment, carved with ancient writing. It helped historians learn how to read Egyptian hieroglyphics.*

▼ *Granite formations by the sea can form beautiful landscapes.*

# STICKING OUT

Extrusive igneous rocks form on Earth's surface. They are formed from the lava that has erupted from volcanoes. This rock cools and hardens faster than intrusive igneous rock. The crystallization process is fast so these rocks are usually fine-grained and have a glassy appearance.

## QUICK TO COOL

In some extrusive igneous rocks, such as pumice, air and other gases get trapped in the lava as it cools. The gas bubbles leave holes in the rock when it hardens.

## QUICKER TO COOL

Other extrusive rocks, including the volcanic glass obsidian, form when lava meets water and cools extremely fast. Obsidian cools so quickly that it does not have mineral crystals. Obsidian is found in Mexico, Iceland, and Japan.

▶ Glass-like obsidian was used to create early mirrors.

## ON THE BEACH

✳ In Hawaii, there are beaches made up of black sand. They are formed from **eroded** basalt, an extrusive igneous rock.

▼ Trapped air bubbles in pumice make the rock light enough to float.

## COOLING OFF

When basaltic lava cools, it sometimes forms hexagonal, or six-sided, columns. The Giant's Causeway in Northern Ireland is made up of more than 40,000 hexagonal columns.

◀ *The Giant's Causeway is the most popular tourist attraction in Northern Ireland.*

▼ *When hot lava enters the ocean it creates huge steam clouds.*

## JUST LIKE GLASS

(This activity needs adult supervision.)

**You will need:**

- 1 cup of sugar
- 1 cup of water
- cooking pot
- metal tray
- stove

Put the sugar and water into the pot. Heat the mixture on the stove until the sugar dissolves in the water. Pour this hot mixture onto the cold metal tray and let it cool down. Notice how it cools into a glass-like sheet. Obsidian forms in a similar way.

# STAYING INSIDE

**I**ntrusive igneous rocks form underground. Magma cools slowly and hardens into rock while it is still underground. Sometimes magma hardens into an enormous mass of igneous rock deep underground. This is called a batholith.

## UNDERGROUND ROCK MASSES

The granite peaks of the Sierra Nevada Mountain Range are the exposed parts of a huge batholith under the range. There is an even larger batholith under the Coast Range in British Columbia, Canada. The Coast Range is a string of mountain ranges along the Pacific coast of North America.

▼ *Underground forces continue to uplift the Sierra Nevada batholith, even today.*

## FILLING THE SPACE

**You will need:**
- two slices of cheese
- squeezable ketchup

Place two cheese slices on top of each other. Open up the nozzle of a squeezable ketchup bottle and push the nozzle between the cheese slices. Apply pressure to the ketchup bottle. Watch how the ketchup oozes its way out of the space between the cheese slices. In this way, the ketchup is like lava and the space between the cheese slices is a crack in Earth's crust.

## PARDON THE INTRUSION

✳ Intrusive igneous rocks include granite, gabbro, diorite, and pegmatite. Pegmatite is known for being extremely coarse-grained.

◀ *A fragment of granite showing coarse-grained texture*

## SILLS AND DIKES

Sometimes magma seeps into a horizontal crack in Earth's crust. As the magma spreads into the crack, it may form a flat sheet of volcanic rock, which is called a **sill**. A dike forms when magma flows into a vertical crack and hardens.

▲ *Basalt dike in granite*

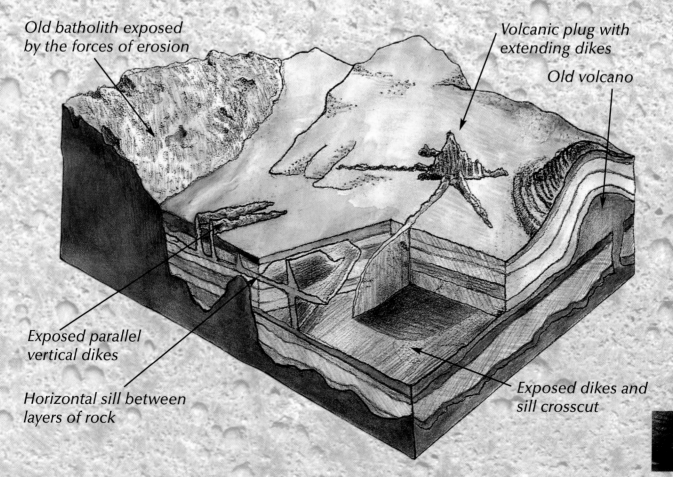

*Old batholith exposed by the forces of erosion*

*Volcanic plug with extending dikes*

*Old volcano*

*Exposed parallel vertical dikes*

*Horizontal sill between layers of rock*

*Exposed dikes and sill crosscut*

17

# BIG-TIME BASALT

The most common extrusive igneous rock is basalt. The lava that forms basalt is heavy, dark-colored, and dense. Basaltic rock is black or very dark gray because it contains high amounts of the minerals iron and magnesium.

## BASALT PILLOWS

Pillow basalt forms when hot lava flows into ocean water and cools quickly. These "pillows" can range in size from a couple of inches to several meters long.

## BED TIME

* There are large beds of basalt near the Columbia River and Snake River in the western United States. There is also basalt on the ocean floor. It is covered in mud and other sediment.

▼ *This pillow texture is very common in underwater basaltic flows.*

## BASALT WALLS

People use basalt in the construction of buildings and cobblestone walkways. They also make statues from basalt.

▶ *Dark gray basalt lava was used to build the façade of the Museum of Modern Art in Vienna, Austria.*

## HARD TO HANDLE

(This activity needs adult supervision.)

**You will need:**
- piece of wax
- cooking pot
- bowl
- 1 cup cold water

Melt the wax in the pot. Put the cold water into the bowl. Pour the melted wax into the bowl of cold water. Notice how the wax hardens into a pillow-like shape. Pillow basalt forms the same way when hot lava flows into an ocean.

## BASALT PIPES

Thick basaltic lava sometimes cools and cracks to form large columns called columnar basalt. Organ Pipes National Park in Victoria, Australia, contains columnar basalt that looks like enormous organ pipes.

▼ *Basalt columns that look like organ pipes can also be found in the Svartifoss waterfall in Skaftafell National Park, Iceland.*

19

# GREAT GRANITE

Granite is one of the most common igneous rocks on Earth. It is a coarse-grained rock that is made up mainly of the minerals feldspar and quartz. There are also smaller amounts of darker-colored minerals, such as biotite and hornblende, in granite. People use granite as a building stone because it is extremely hard and **durable**.

## GOOD FOR BUILDING

Granite contains large mineral crystals that can be light gray, white, pink, pale yellow, or black. For thousands of years, people have **quarried** slabs of granite and used it to construct buildings, monuments, tombstones, and other structures.

▼ Granite slabs like these are used in construction.

## BATHOLITH

✱ Granite forms huge batholiths that were originally below Earth's surface.

▼ Granite comes in a range of colors, from pink to gray or sometimes black.

▼ Biotite is a mineral that can be found in granite.

## FAMOUS GRANITE STRUCTURES

The Mount Rushmore National Memorial in South Dakota is made mainly from granite. Many public and commercial buildings have granite flooring. Some people have polished granite countertops and floor tiles in their homes because granite is especially durable and beautiful.

▲ Some kitchen counters are made of granite.

▼ Mount Rushmore National Memorial, near Keystone, South Dakota, is a monumental granite sculpture featuring the heads of former United States presidents.

21

# THE MINERAL EFFECT

Igneous rocks are made up of minerals. Minerals are natural substances found on Earth—there are thousands of different minerals. They form when elements in a gas or a liquid crystallize into a solid. There are about 100 known elements.

## MORE ABOUT MINERALS

When magma below Earth's surface is pushed up toward the crust, it cools and certain elements begin to crystallize. Different minerals crystallize at different temperatures and amounts of pressure. Certain combinations of elements form different minerals. For example, the mineral quartz is made up of silicon and oxygen.

## APOPHYLLITE

Apophyllite is a mineral found in basalt and other igneous rocks. Its crystals can be pale pink, white, green, or yellow.

*Apophyllites form interesting crystals, which make them very popular as collector's minerals.*

## CRAZY CRYSTALS

(This activity needs adult supervision.)

Make your own crystals

### You will need:

- paper clip
- pencil
- small piece of string
- 1 cup water
- teaspoon
- cooking pot
- medium-sized glass jar
- 1/2 cup salt
- stove

Tie a paper clip to one end of the string and tie a pencil to the other end of the string. Set aside. Boil the water and pour it into the jar. Dissolve the salt in the boiling water, adding only 1 teaspoon of salt at a time. Lower the paper clip into the water and rest the pencil across the top of the jar. Cover the jar with a paper towel and leave it in a warm place for two or three days. Notice how small crystals begin to form on the paper clip and on the string.

◄ *Amethyst is a variety of quartz and a well-known gem.*

## FAMOUS CONDUCTOR

✳ Copper is a mineral found in igneous rocks. It is an excellent **conductor** of heat and electricity.

◄ *Copper was one of the first metals used by humans.*

▶ *Rose quartz is often carved into figures.*

### QUIRKY QUARTZ

Quartz is one of the most common minerals in Earth's crust. People can identify most minerals by looking at or testing various properties, including the color, hardness, or **transparency** of the mineral.

### MINERAL GROUPS

There are different groups of minerals. The largest and most common group of minerals is called silicates. Silicates are made up mostly of the elements oxygen and silicon. Certain silicates are involved in the formation of rocks.

# SUPER SILICATES

**S**ilicates are the largest group of minerals. Most igneous rocks are made up of 95 percent silicates. Rock forming silicates include feldspar, quartz, olivine, garnet, and mica. There are more than 1,000 different silicates.

## SILICATES AROUND YOU

Silica is one silicate that is known for its hardness and is used to make many kinds of glass including window glass, drinking glasses, and glass bottles. It is the most abundant mineral in Earth's crust.

## SILICATES AROUND YOU

Feldspar is another type of silicate mineral. It is used in **ceramics**. Feldspar's crystals can be white, gray, pink, or brown.

▲ Feldspar is a common raw material in the making of pottery.

▼ Garnets have been used since the **Bronze Age** as gemstones.

▼ Human use of mica dates back to prehistoric times.

▼ Olivine is one of the most common minerals on Earth.

▼ Smoky quartz is a brown to black variety of quartz.

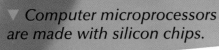
▼ *Computer microprocessors are made with silicon chips.*

## SUPER SILICON

Most semiconductor chips in computers are created with silicon. You may have heard expressions like "Silicon Valley" and the "silicon economy." It is because silicon is the heart of any electronic device.

▼ *The major ingredient for glassmaking is silica in the form of sand.*

## ROUGH STUFF

Sandpaper is made of silicon carbide, which is a combination of minerals that are almost as hard as diamonds.

▶ *Sandpaper made of silicon carbide can be used to polish both wet and dry surfaces.*

# QUALITY QUARTZ

Quartz is the second-most abundant mineral in Earth's crust. Quartz is one of the hardest silicate minerals and is made almost entirely of silica. There are many colored varieties of quartz including rose quartz, citrine quartz, milky quartz, and smoky quartz. Pure quartz is colorless and transparent.

## QUARTZ JEWELRY

In Europe and the Middle East, people use quartz to make jewelry and carvings. People use milky quartz to make beads, **cameos**, and rings. A cameo is a carved gem with a design on it. Some quartz crystals are big enough to cut into gemstones, which can then be placed into necklaces, rings, or bracelets.

▼ *Quartz in small sand-sized grains can accumulate to form sand dunes.*

## BIG DEPOSIT

✳ There are large deposits of quartz in Arkansas. The quartz **belt** is about 149 miles (240 km) long and 15 miles (24 km) wide. It extends southwest from Little Rock, Arkansas, all the way to northern Oklahoma.

▼ *Expertly cut agate mineral can be turned into a cameo gem.*

## IT'S NOT ICE!

❋ For hundreds of years, early civilizations believed that quartz crystals were permanently frozen pieces of ice.

◀ Colorless and transparent, pure quartz is called a rock crystal.

▶ Rose quartz in crystal form is called pink quartz.

◀ Citrine quartz ranges from a pale yellow to brown.

▶ Milky quartz is the most common variety of quartz and can be found almost anywhere.

▲ People have used precious stones and gems as jewelry throughout history.

# THE HUMAN TOUCH

People have been studying igneous rocks for hundreds of years. They are fascinated by the behavior and histories of these and other types of rocks. Scientists who study rocks to find information about the history of Earth and its life-forms are called **geologists**.

## ROCKIN' IT

Igneous rocks are among the oldest rocks on Earth. They were created by volcanoes over the course of millions of years. Igneous rocks are still forming today and they will continue to form for millions of years to come. Every time there is a volcanic eruption, new igneous rocks begin to form.

▶ *A great way to learn about rocks is to attend a geology summer camp.*

▶ *Rock quarries are often huge holes cut into mountains.*

## DUSTY AND DIRTY

✽ Dust from quarries is a major source of air pollution.

## QUARRIES: GOOD AND BAD

Quarrying is a form of mining. People mine for large deposits of rocks, such as granite. The rocks are blasted with explosives, which can cause noise pollution and air pollution.

## FILLING UP

As people dig deeper and deeper mines, they use up all the rocks and minerals in an area. These empty quarries are then used as **landfill** sites for garbage and other waste. Landfills cause pollution and can harm the habitats of plants and animals.

◄ *Old quarries turned into landfills can pose a danger to wild animals.*

▼ *Explosions in quarries create a lot of dust that can cause air pollution.*

## TOO MUCH

✳ Today some countries are studying the environmental impact of granite mining to help them decide if they should put restrictions on granite exports.

# GLOSSARY

**batholith** Igneous rock that has hardened into an enormous mass deep underground

**belt** An area formed by similar processes containing rocks of similar composition

**Bronze Age** A period between 3500 BC and 1200 BC when bronze was used for metalworking

**cameos** A carving or small sculpture in stone

**ceramics** Products, such as porcelain or brick, made from a mineral

**conductor** A substance that allows heat to pass through it

**continents** The vast areas of land on Earth; The continents are North America, South America, Asia, Europe, Africa, Australia, and Antarctica.

**crust** The outer layer of Earth

**crystallize** To form crystals

**durable** Describing something that lasts a long time

**eroded** Describing something that has worn away from the action of water or wind

**extrusive rocks** Rocks formed from lava that cools

**fault line** A separation or crack in Earth's crust where two tectonic plates meet

**geologist** Scientist who studies the history of Earth and its life as recorded in rocks

**intrusive rocks** Rocks formed by the solidification of magma below the surface of Earth

**landfill** A place where garbage is buried between layers of dirt

**lava** Melted rock that comes from a volcano

**lava flow** Masses of molten rock that pour onto Earth's surface during a volcanic eruption

**magma** Molten rock within Earth

**mantle** The layer of Earth between the crust and the core

**minerals** Chemicals that occur naturally on Earth in the form of crystals

**pumice** A very light gray stone formed from lava that cools in the air

**quarried** To dig stone from a quarry

**sediment** Material within a liquid that settles to the bottom

**sill** A horizontal sheet of igneous rock intruded between older rock

**tectonic plates** Massive slabs of moving rock beneath the ground

**transparency** The quality or state of being sheer enough to see through

# MORE INFORMATION

## FURTHER READING

*Igneous Rock.*
   Rebecca Faulkner. Raintree Freestyle 1st Edition. 2007.

*Rocks and Minerals: Igneous Rocks.*
   Melissa Stewart. Heinemann Library Hardbacks. 2004.

*Granite and Other Igneous Rocks.*
   Chris Pellant and Helen Pellant. Gareth Stevens Publishing. 2007.

*Igneous Rocks: From Fire to Stone.*
   Darlene R. Stille. Compass Point Books. 2008.

*Igneous Rocks and the Rock Cycle.*
   Joanne Mattern. PowerKids Press. 2006.

*Diamonds and Gemstones.*
   Ron Edwards and Lisa Dickie. Crabtree Publishing Company. 2004.

*Minerals.*
   Adrianna Morganelli. Crabtree Publishing Company. 2004.

## WEBSITES

**RocksForKids**
www.rocksforkids.com/

**Geology for Kids**
www.kidsgeo.com/geology-for-kids/

**Mineralogy for Kids**
www.minsocam.org/MSA/K12/K_12.html

**GNS Science**
www.gns.cri.nz/kids/

**How Rocks Are Formed**
www.rocksforkids.com/RFK/howrocks.html

# INDEX